Feel Me

A Poet Writes of Love, Lust, Loss & Life

Alee J.

FEEL ME: A POET SPEAKS OF LOVE, LUST, LOSS & LIFE

ISBN 978-1-7362277-6-3 (Paperback)

Designed and Published by King's Daughter Publishing
Indian Trail, North Carolina 28079
www.KingsDaughterPublishing.com

Printed in the United States of America.

Dedication
Acknowledgements

∞ **LOVE** ∞

About Me 9
Availability 10
Be 11
Being in Love 12
Can You… 13
Destiny 15
Feel Me 16
Gentle Expressions 17
Glide 19
Hear Ye, Hear Ye 20
Kinetic Energy 21
Learned Behaviors 22
My Gem, My Jewel 23
Old Fri 24
Raised Bars 25
Real Confirmation 26
Rear View 27
Right Hand, Left Stand 28
Tell the Story 29
Telling Times 31
The Key 32
Tonight 33
Total Connection 34
Where Bruises Come From 35
Woman of Valor 37
Wonderful Vibes 38

∞ LUST ∞

Allowance 40
Dew Time 41
Dick Drunk 42
Learn Me Something 43
Let's Bone 44
Main Vein 46
Open Wide 47
The Vise 49

∞ LOSS ∞

Barely Home 51
Broken 52
Crying River 53
Don't Waste My Breath 54
Impressions 55
Innocence 56
Meet Me 58
My Worth 59
No More 60
Reality Bytes 61

∞ LIFE ∞

A Pain 63
Audacity 64
Be the Dream 65
Bounce 66
Captured Feelings 67
Choosy Losers 68
Dreaming 69
Experiences 70
For Real or For Fake 71
Happy Happy, Joy Joy 72
Haters 73
Inspiration 74
O.P.P. 75
Personalities 76

Quiet Storm 77
Roll Modeling 78
Self Sync 79
Solace 80
Take a Breath 81
That's Enough 82
Thicker than Blood 83
Twisted Turns 84
Vocals Needed 85
Warm Up 86
What Kind 87
Who am I? 88
Why Me? 89

About the Author 90

I dedicate this book to my internal freedom.

Giving thanks to All that is Pure and Positive in my life that allows for such gift of expression.

Doris, my aunt: Your encouragements have always come with the push for bettering myself and having no bounds. For that, I love, cherish and thank you — to infinity.

My Daughter, Zharia: Thank you for being you & allowing me to view a version of myself. Your birth supplied me with the patience I needed to live this through. I LOVE YOU.

Aunt Nett, Uncle Johnny & Phyllis: Thank you for listening, proof-reading, giving motivation & allowing me to witness the surprise and awe on your faces, I have nothing but Love.

Besties: Keba, my girlfriend, my partner in crime, my Ace Boon Coon…THANK YOU! There is truly only one of you. Plus, the world couldn't handle two! Carolyn, 20 years is a really long time for me to consider and call someone a sister/best friend, and that alone speaks volumes no words can express. Thank you & I love you girl.

Thanks to all the **Men Motivation**, because in this life we have to take the good with the bad. So, thanks of all kinds are in short order, not to be repeated.

A special thanks to S. Kristi Douglas of King's Daughter Publishing. Your ideas made my vision a Reality! You are truly the Best Damn Publisher in my book & I thank you for your patience and open heart.

For everyone that I absolutely love & didn't name, there's just entirely too many of you. I thank you for the support and continuing to aim for our true happiness.

Love ♡

About Me♡

I'm kind-hearted.
My spirit is free.
I CAN BE LOUD A$$ HELL!
But I'm the fun
You wanna be.
My problem is—
I love BIG.
I love *whole*.
When I love, I love from parts of my soul.
That makes me something to hold!
About me…
I don't wanna be a novelty!
I won't settle for anything less
Than your treasure chest.

Availability

When is it okay to express my emotions to you?
If your answer is, "Whenever."
Why then, when I try, do you make a motion that shuts me down?

No specific words such as that are spoken,
But loudly demonstrated.
Body gestures and movements
Leave me to believe that you don't have
The Mental time available to me.
Then am I wrong to mentally bond with another willing soul?

To not be perceived as "emotional"
For having emotions you want expressed
Is to say you are free while allowing chains—attached.

Something has *got* to give!

Be♡

Be with me throughout the rest of my days.
Release the apprehension,
Give this love your solid attention.
To all the details left behind,
It wasn't a plan…it's by design.
Stay with me, relax and let's lay.
Lay down your guard, I'm not here just for play.
Play music that leaves the body weak
With emotion from deep inside.
I'll ride the tide.
Dive in the water, 'til it runs clear.
And seeps in places no one's ever been.
Give me space to sit and spin.
I'll make you the winner in the end.
The room is clear.
The space is free
Now, for you to
Express your desire
To be with me.

Being in Love

Being in Love is sometimes thought to be a HOAX.
You can't touch it…Oh wait, yes you can.
You can't smell it…Oh wait, yes you can.
You can't hear it…Oh wait, yes you can.
You can't taste it…Oh but, yes you can.

Love is seen on the faces of all happy people.
When you hear sweet words delivered on a bed of roses,
that's Love.
Touching that feels like feathers on your skin.
Barely making a connection, but still causing you to get—
the shivers.
It's smooth like honey, sticky and sweet, while going down,
Coating everything it makes contact with.

And, oh the smell…
Imagine the sweetest sex, dripping with desire,
Floating on a cloud of Pure Ecstasy.
Mmmm the Smell!

Once you've experienced being in Love…
Truly in Love…

Make sure to never come down.

Can You...

Can you love me tender?
Can you see me through?
Can you open your mind, heart and soul?
Can you let this love come to you?
Even from my eyes
I'm trying to see your view...
And from there –
The sight is clear!

But can you...
Open your mind – and see?
My view comes from over here.

We can't even begin
To really, truly begin
Until you open up and let my view in.
What I say and feel
Should count to more than just me.
When the woman you're describing me to be
Is actually your self-imagery.
In this relationship
It's supposed to be "We."

We need to walk this bridge
From both ends to close this gap.
Because, at this point – if the ropes get much tighter
We know they are bound to snap!

FEEL ME

Snap in or snap out—
That fate will not fall on me.
So…
Can you…
Work with me
To build our "we?"

Destiny♡

Destiny.
What is My Destiny?

Prove to me
That you're meant to be
My Destiny.

Throughout my life
It hasn't been sweet.
So, what would make you think
To treat me like
I would just know?

If Destiny didn't show me the path,
Why am I suffering the wrath
Of decisions made in haste?

Destiny.
Teach me not to chase
The opposite of my dreams
And waste what is meant to be
The Time of My Life!

Destiny.
For making this one count.
Because, without a doubt
I will stand tall and shout,
"Thank you for being
My Destiny!"

Feel Me

Sway with my soul.
Sing the rhythm that's yours to own.
Own me
Like only you.
Be the way you know I need and sway with me.
Let the waves carry us.
Teach me what I don't know and we can learn together.
Learn to laugh, to cry
Learn to just be.
I have many ways to express being me,
So, let life sway your reasons my way.
So we can just
Sway.

Gentle Expressions

Talk to me in the tones you like.
Don't fight my words –
Let's have a conversation.

It's the closure you wanted,
Just not expressed in your desire.

Yes, I know it's hard.
But one can't do both parts for long.
That's not how we started this song!

Flip flopping on words, like I got tripped jumping rope.
You're making me lose hope
And my hope, floats.
I've done all I'm willing to give into this.
Feeling alone.
'Cuz without your Soul Deposit,
This house doesn't feel like our home.

You were more dominant.
You were supposed to guide.
Now, I'll guide my slide,
Riding, wondering,
How did this even begin?

My Soul
Told me we could win!

FEEL ME

Guess I
Wasn't in your plan.

That's why
I have to take this stand
And feel my expression.

Glide♡

I never knew that tunnel of ecstasy existed.
I had no idea where you were headed.
Gliding through with all the ownership needed,
To possess this space.
A space that has elevated the connection.
Making your presence known.
Enjoying the sweet slide, provided
Knowing it's yours and yours alone.
Rubbing along the path; tapping out the tune
To sound of a G note.
Demanding full access,
To the IOU personally wrote.
This space has such peace,
Within its midst, it's savory.
Never being able and quite enjoying the freedom allowed
To Glide.
With the ease of one in their true essence.
So, thank you for allowing me in your sanctum of solace...
To Glide.

Hear Ye, Hear Ye

Hear ye, hear ye!
For what I say is true.
I am learning valuable lessons
From this producer at his booth.
Writing out feelings when good at expression,
Makes for one Hell of a session!
The flow and vibe, dance to the music so sweet.
Finally glad, to be created from his heat.
A heat to burn.
A heat to soothe.
A heat with such groove and bite,
You can't help but move & say, "Damn! That's tight!"
This description is not given to recognize.
This is the steps taken at building a franchise.
One of love, success and all that is pure!
For all those around and willing to endure
So...
Hear ye, hear ye!
For I speak the truth.
I have learned a valuable lesson
From this man – at his booth!

Kinetic Energy♡

When someone calls you spoiled—
Is it automatically meant as an insult?
Well for me, I am declaring such.
I Am Spoiled!
When I return home for the day,
My daddy has dinner waiting for me
As soon as I'm out of the shower.
If there's anything I'm needing or wanting from him,
It's like we are synced.
He's always there when I need him to ease my mind.
And pops up when he's strong on my mind.
To know that you have finally gotten it right!
Not that's it's the words that make it happen.
When you feel the completion and your hearts finally beats one rhythm.
That's when you know you have found the one person
Destined to live out this life with you.
This kinetic energy attaches itself
When two destined souls
Make their connection complete.

Learned Behaviors♡

When expressions are given or elicited from you,
You often wonder
How did this happen?
It almost feels as if you have no control.
As if your body was borrowed for a bit.
When those said emotions have you feeling some kinda wonderful,
Why question it?
Is it in our nature to question life or is it a learned behavior?
A behavior learned by many, needing to be lost by most.
So, why fight it?
Fight the emotions that flow
Leaving a lingering effect?
Feel what you need to feel!
Absorb all the goodness that's aimed at you
And. Just. Feel.
Feel the feelings.
Find your way!
And for once, allow yourself to get HIT!

My Gem, My Jewel♡

There is usually a favorite gem,
A jewel that speaks to one's heart.
Well, my gem, my jewel,
That's my favorite part.
Although it isn't a stone,
It was shaped, molded and treated with such care–
A care that has it ever-forming;
Forming with a thirst of particular edges not yet seen before.
When I see the way it shines, once pressure is applied,
It blinds the natural eye.
A shine so bright it brings tears to my eyes
And so much joy to my heart.

So,
To answer the elated question
Of what my gem, my jewel, my favorite part is…
Look up, look out.
You're bound to see
This great life I've found having my Mini Me.

Mommy loves you.

Old Fri♡

Old Fri is not a food, unless you're tailored to my flavor of chocolate.
My Old Fri is 50 plus in age, but ageless everywhere else.
Old Fri is knowledgeable with lots to say on many subjects.
Old Fri gives laughs from silliness, moans from loving, depth from conversation, and variety for life.
Not my life alone, but our future together.
You see, what you need to grasp is that…
My Old Fri is mine.
Built to match my taste and seasoned from my love.
Old Fri has done what no other has been able to achieve.
Old Fri has become irreplaceable.

Way to go, Old Fri.

Raised Bars♡

Ding!
The bell rings – starting warm as it goes.
That liquid fire feeling spreading itself into every crevice
of my being.
The embers inside, traveling, aren't meant for destruction
But to comfort and heal all the cracks left behind.
Blood pumping in my ears;
Switching up the heartbeat;
Creating a rhythmic hum
For the Transitional Phase you've entered.
Did you not read the instructions?
Did you miss the signs?
How would one know what to look for
If the eyes looking doesn't know for what to search?
You see, a magnitude of emotions follow every decision made.
It can take a while to get your tuners equalized.
But oh, when you do!
You will have a feeling of elevation.
New in every way.
You have just
Raised the bar.

Real Confirmation

When you need to hear that "You are Important."
When you need to get that sexy look, with a wink…
When the phone calls end with no terms of endearment…

Are these the things that are claimed to make a person feel weak or insecure?
Needing and wanting confirmation from loved ones we hold dear means that we love them.
We love the way they make us feel when we are in their presence.
The sound of their voice;
The touch of their skin;
The confirmation that they are there and that they are REAL.
Real honest.
Real confirmations.
Real dreams.
Real life!
A confirmation could change a person's day, week, year…life.
Confirmation - Confirmed.

Rear View

I need to be loved tenderly.
I require love that's pure.
Can you show your treasured side
And will it reassure?
Reassure, so I know our time wasn't wasted
And our energy has grown.
Grown to see a life together
With us in our own zone.
What we want now, should top
Each of our individual lists
To cover all the bases that were previously missed.
Making this time count;
Spreading honesty throughout this review.
Waving goodbye to the negativity
In my Rear View.

Right Hand, Left Stand♡

Everyone has a right hand, literally!
But the kind of right hand I'm speaking of is the kind you never have to find.
That's always there when you need it, no matter what you need it for.
That's a very Big title to have; to carry.

Many always say that they are in fact a Right Hand.
The real question is…
Do you deserve it? Does it deserve you?
Do you deserve such loyalty? Are you loyal?
The questions asked aren't for fun or even to equal the score.
It's merely questioning your examination of yourself.
It's an internal review.

Now, high five with your left hand.
See how strong that is?
Well it doesn't take a wiz to know, that left hand
Is his.
Acting as a missing part, when you're in need
To stabilize the foundation by adding his steed.
It's the left to your right and vice versa for him.
Showing the full force, behind having four limbs.
Getting the job done Right
Once and for all, they say.
But having that left, to my right
Is REQUIRED, for me to stay.

Tell the Story

Be for me what you want.
Don't Front!

Call me when you have the space.
Let's not waste precious time
To indulge in this purple
While we whine our tale in a circle.

Get a grip.
Tell a story.
Don't worry
About the future or the past
We gone last.

Create in me a fire
That burns of hidden desires
And dreams fulfilled in rhyme.
Spare me your time
And tell the story

About the glory days
And the many different ways
You grew to be a man.
Show me the plan.
Laid at your feet
I'll take a seat
And listen to all you have to say

FEEL ME

Any time, Any day, Any way you want.
Don't Front!

Listen to me sing off-key.
Open my vocals
And see if you made a change.
Do I now sound strange?

Fall into me on your worst day.
I promise I won't lead you astray
From the joy within our grasp.

Don't let the past dictate your life.
Reclaim the Power.
Deny the Strife.
Stop the Stray.
Find your way.
And be who YOU Desire – Today
And just
Tell Your Story!

Telling Times♡

Don't make it work for me.
We gotta put the work In
To win for us.

Meant to stand
All kinds of weather.
Our success is to be gained
Together.
We both know better!
Better than what is being shown;
Blowing hot at every bend.
Respect isn't a given, it should be earned.
So, let's mend these split ends and
Get our roots back golden
To cherish this precious egg
Placed in our care;
To handle
Closing this divide;
Making the decision to decide
That this is between You & Me
About – Us.

The Key

I've had relationships to boot,
But a comparison could not be had.
One thing is for certain--good is good and bad is bad.
Good – is when he serves you with that special smile.
While Bad—Bad sends you to get his dinner—preordered in style.
You are his maid, his housekeeper and hoe to the nine.
But would Good allow his Queen to feel less than his dime?
Worth all that a man should provide and nurture what she needs;
Which should be considered when—Bad is out with another steed.
See, Bad, he can't recognize the worth in one, when his appetite is his spice.
It also makes for a lonely man in this quest called life.
Now, Good – Good will flourish in life and love, to the point of absolute bliss.
You see, he has learned the key,
The most important piece...
That having one dime
Is wealth, beyond belief!

Atmosphere so thick that our normal breaths seem heavy.
Heavy to the point of being from one room to the next.
How to lessen the load of thoughts so big they occupy the whole space
While strengths and accomplishments are being hurled like daggers.
Finding the space to move out of the way.
Having tried to clear the air...
All the while knowing the next moves aren't yours to make.
Fully submerging in the submissive nature requested of you in this area of life.
"Breathe easy – turning tides are in your favor,"
Says all the energy surrounding me tonight.

Total Connection

Electricity buzzing through my veins.
Nerves bouncing with barely controlled excitement.
Hairs on their tips, stretching towards the source.
Muscles jumping with joy, like a kid at Christmas.
These are the feelings of a Total Connection!
I never knew such a thing, but as I'm prone to reading,
I could only imagine such vibes,
Such feeling that one word would not do justice
To capture all of what happens.
Now, I'm done reading those books.
I'm only just realizing that
I traded my imaginary world of
Real true love for the real thing!
I now feel the way I've dreamt of feeling.
I'm being loved the way I deserve.
All these have come to me at the moment I least expected
And most needed.
I have JOY!
Joy down in my soul so deep, that it's
Saturated into my very being.

Where Bruises Come From

People feel that marriage is the key to all happiness.
But I know this to be untrue.
So, let me explain from my eyes so you can have a view.
You see, I've done this dance with more than a couple;
Actually three.

#1 – had his hands full of a spunky little me.
A true grasp of the woman I was becoming, not even he could see.
Most times I was amazed and I had all kinds of high hopes,
But hopes alone can't quench certain desires – even if you tie them with rope.

#2 – was virile and exuded such strength that I thought I was hit with Cupid's arrow twice!
After feeling like damaged property, I was shocked and thrilled that he came with such spice.
But expectations can get the best of you when learning the weakness in others leaves you hollow.
It's because of these actions divorce papers had to follow.

Now #3 – doesn't deserve any kind of time, just keeping it Real.
But something I learned from him was…
My life, my time…is mine!
Mine to do, mine to see and mine to go about as I please.
Not allowing him, with his issues, to make me feel like a sleaze!

FEEL ME

You see, I don't break this down to express my doubts of Love or Marriage.
Dragging old baggage around is not the purpose of my course.
It's quite the opposite, in fact.
Getting all this out and being able to cleanse my palate
Grants me the ability to start again…with a clean under carriage.
It allows me a kind of rebirth
Given to me after each divorce.

Woman of Valor♡

I love you more than Chuck loves chocolate cake.
And even though you are super creative,
I love you more than anything you could make.
You are to me a special spirit that runs, wild and free, but also a bit tamed.
"Doris" was rightfully given to you, so you were perfectly named.
You have made yourself important and someone to be adored.
Even if you don't always know where things are stored,
In this quest called life, it's a journey you face with such optimism and goals.
In the passing of people, you don't just shake hands or hug, you touch souls—
Souls that want to stay and be by your side
Which only made your circle grow very wide.
So, when more plans are made and you finally decide from what state you wish to sip shade
Just remember, gems shine in all lights!

Wonderful Vibes

When the ordinary job of opening your eyes
Represents a mouthful of chocolate to a cho-co-holic;
A taste so good, that it leaves the soul sweet.
When all you desire is being in the wonderful vibes that you helped create,
You just want to saturate in this oasis with your mate to the next destination.
This, this is the feeling of a true home.
A home made with all the ingredients needed for growth and dreams being fulfilled,
All while smelling like seasoned steaks on the grill.
A path lined up so neat,
You can't help but stand and take this heat!

Lust

Allowance♡

I'm smooth like honey, sticky and sweet;
Coating everything in contact.
Talk dirty, baby, smack my cheeks.
Show me where you signed that fat contract.
I'm dick drunk with desire, to wrap
My heritage around your heat.
So, if describing my state of mind is hard to hear
Then you should stand to your feet–
Feet built to match my speed,
With the cream and cherry on top.
Control is what I'm seeking.
Just finding the strength to stop;
Staring at what's already coated
And feeling quite proud
At the things we accomplish
When allowed.

Dew Time

Grab the snacks and I'll get the cover.
I plan to do more than just hover.

Time alone ain't no joke.
So, slide my way so I can poke.

Suck it hard and pinch the tip.
Make yo' tongue do that dip.

Fast – slow, find your motion.
You got that magic potion.

Push – pull, let's tug of war.
And keep going 'til we both score.

I always got what you need,
Follow and I'll feed my seed.

Give me space to sit and spin,
And we'll see how long it takes to win.

The prize in the end, was worth the start,
That's how I won your heart.

Dick Drunk♡

I know this sounds like a mouthful
Or something of an illicit nature,
But it's actually a description.
It's describing a state of mind.
See, this level of drunkenness
CANNOT be gauged by liquor alone.
This has no equal!
Being in this state will have you stumbling around,
Looking for an anchor.
Needing stability of something to steady your wobbling legs,
fuzzy head, tingling skin,
And a breath you're desperately attempting to catch.

If this sounds tragic, believe me when I say,
It's Not!
Now that the feeling has been felt,
I don't believe it's a state of being dick drunk
But being Dick Dared!
Daring the Drunkenness
To capture me
In its euphoric grasp...

So, here I stand,
With lube in hand
Daring the Dick to make me
Drunk again
And again!

Learn Me Something♡

Show me.
Teach me.
Learn me something.
Give me instructions
Down to your full pleasure.
Teach me,
Please me.
Push my buttons.
Show me where to start.
You set the mark.

Your All-man-joy (almond joy) is my pleasure.
So, lay back and
Treasure this
Like it's the first time.
Watch the shine!

Slick, Tip – n – slide, my favorite fun ride
Like a surfer catching the big tide!

You
Are
Mine!

The declaration is made clear, "Mon Cheri."
Close the eyes that Need to see
All we could become

Staying in tune
While beating on those Bad Azz Drums.

Let's Bone

Fly away, swim free.
Share your love with me.
Let's grind to the tenth power.
Climb this tower
So I can shower you with gifts
Of appreciation, the likes
You've never known.
Yes, let's bone
Til' we both pass out.
Whew, this shit so good,
I just wanna shout!
Fuck it all!
Let's run away
To a zone
That's ours and ours alone
Where we can just bone.
In a space that clings
Long after applied.
Others have tried,
To unlock the core
That keeps you wanting more.
More Love.
More Kiss.
More of what you miss
The most!
So, now
Let me take my post

And give you a
Proper.
Hostess.
Greeting.
I will supply ALL your feedings,
Including whatever you crave.
We can save the freaky for later
Let the moment savor
And preserve the flavor
Of a combination
So Right.
Who are we to fight?
This growing pressure with no measure
Of the greatness inside.
So, take me for the Ride of a Lifetime.

Main Vein

Fuck me like you mean it.
Don't spare me the pain.
Pain verses pleasure, now that's my main vein.
Gaining mounds of joy, when Mr. Goodbar dives deep.
Adding twix played, that tootsie rolled yo ass to sleep.
That's why the games we play, once behind closed doors,
Are specifically designed to keep you wanting more.
So, scream like a bitch, or shut up and moan.
You know what time it is when Daddy comes home.
Home to the trigger that controls so much heat.
Even the animal inside has to
Control the need to beat
His pussy in a fashion so slick
And watch as the ride
Slide it Up and Down
From the base to the
Tip of this Dick!

Now go, wet your lips
Then love the dome
And come show Daddy
All that I own.
Tease him
Please him.
Shit, turn him OUT!
Now, that's what I'm talkin' 'bout.

Open Wide♡

Open wide.
Say, "Ahhh."
Stick your tongue all the way out.
Lick those lips.
Clear that throat…
It's time to Deep Throat.
We talk so long and clear
With no words expressed,
But a language in its own rights
That would win any test.
Searching corners for new discoveries to find.
Knowing fun is being had, evenly on both sides.
Quick! Change positions, movements.
Let's make this lion–growl.
Repeatedly challenging his boys on the prowl.
Tie him down.
Don't hurt the meat.
All desires scream at once.
Hold 'em tight, go slow.
Don't trip, this could take all night.
Sometime is how I like it, so that would be just fine;
How I like to explore.
Lips.
Tongue.
Titties.
Hands.
Give him all that he can stand.

FEEL ME

He serves his dish so swell, one can't complain.
The image replayed from memory imprinted on my brain.
He places me high.
I mean right at serving level.
Making sure to serve evenly with me on the swivel.
So, open wide.
Say, "Ahhh."
Stick that tongue ALL the way out.
Lick those lips
Clear that throat …
It's time to Deep Throat.

The Vise

Watch me catch you on the run
Giving you clues, making it look fun.
It's going down, you already know.
You might as well put on a show.

For me to sit and watch you wind
Your worries down, before we grind.
Morphing into something, original, in kind
Then, pushing you to the edge of your mind.

Pulling you back down to
Experience that again.
Aiming for a number closer to ten.
Waiting, 'til you hit the ground,
Causing a noiseless sound.

Bound to etch my name in stone.
When you go in your VGP Zone.
Compiling things that are brand new.
Yeah, you know how I do.

Especially when you're around
You start twitching, holding pounds
Of flesh in the rarest cut
With demands like,
"Turn around and let me smack that BUTT!"

Loss

Barely Home

Spare me the pain of your false claims of Love and Loyalty.
Given so much,
I should be ashamed.
Laughing at my soul-baring,
While trying to save face.
Then look me in my eyes
To explain your case.
As... If... I... Could... Care!

To heal me
I finally had to let you go.

So, whether you understand,
You were always in the know.
Your ignorance was bliss,
Only for you.
For me,
It was just too much – lonely
In a house of two.

Broken♡

What happened?

I ask as I'm lying on the ground dazed,
Because I feel as though I've been hit by the World's Biggest Object.

Where did it come from?
I start to ask, then stop.
Why ask the question that's replaying on a repeat spool in my mind?

Checking my body for blood I know should be there
And coming up dry.

Well, why am I hurting so bad then?
Because this pain is radiating from within.

I was shattered from the inside
And not able to reach the pieces.

It's okay.
For me, there is always a missing part.

And like those…

I'm now labeled as
BROKEN.

Crying River♡

Sadness running through my bones
Trying to make me cry.

Making it a crime for my eyes to stay dry.

Let me be –
Don't laugh when I weep!

For my pain to bring you pleasure,
Now that's pretty deep.

Why must I change to fit in your world,
Am I not enough for your lifetime?

Well, having someone's back when they're not around –
That's worth a priceless dime.

Enough so you look through me – to you.
And develop ways to complete the things you need to do.

So, shake off your shoulders and
Hold your head high.

Because
Happiness can also
Make you cry.

Don't Waste My Breath

Don't run and hide
When I shine light
On your traitor ways.

You said it was love you felt.
You said it for months
On different days.

The sorry ways shown, with a smile
Would have put a lesser woman
On the ground.
Or do you think I was in lost and found?

I didn't give my everything
Because it wasn't yours to have.
It was just too much or
So, you had to pass.

In such a cowardice kinda style,
I was very unprepared.
Shock like that doesn't last long.

Once released from your hell
Due to infidelity, was the lie
You ran crying to tell.

Cries of shame you were afraid
Everyone would hear,
Unleashing the bitch inside.
Showing proof to all
Near.

So, take a rest, and don't waste my breath.

Impressions♡

What makes you special enough for someone to stay?
Well, why you asking me? They all ran away.
From too much of me, they couldn't stand.
It's okay if you ask for a helping hand.
You wouldn't be the first to start that trend.
So, no need to pretend to defend
Actions brought about that had you fully submerged
Until you made it to the altar and purged
All those nasty things done in sin,
Only to turn around and do it again.

Your sorrow wasn't real the last few times.
Why wait for the collection plate to add your dimes?
Your input isn't necessary if it's not sincere.
So, stop telling lies to all who will hear
Your woes, aches and you complain.
But guess what? They lied!
It's not all the same.

Innocence♡

Everyone has good days
But bad ones too.
So, hold tight, pay attention
While I share an important one with you.
I was introduced to violence
In one of the worst ways.
Some would compare it to
The freeing of a slave.
A slave of sorts, I had absolutely NO control
Of innocence stolen from me, by a Giant Ass Hole!

Never mind I was a child.
It never seemed to click.
I guess there was just too much space
Between his head and his dick.

Why think about the hurt
When you felt you did no harm?
Smiling in everyone's face
With a nasty ass charm!

When you decide, that anger is your flair
Why punish everyone around, making them aware?

Adding HELL to a home where kids are involved.
Acting like the whelps from beatings would remain unsolved.

In closing, I hope and pray that,
What's meant to happen to you—DOES!!
Because, as far as I can tell,
It never is and it never was.

Meet Me

Irreplaceable.
A huge description one shouldn't let go to the head.
Wanting to build, grow, be better.
That's the true purpose instead.
Everything can't be all my fault,
Even ninety percent of the time.
And in this relationship, if I can see your worth
Then why is it so hard for you to see mine?
I'm a gem, a caring jewel;
Yeah even some stones with no names.
I'm not claiming perfection here, but see,
I'm also not pointing a blame.
This is a plea for care and understanding
Which are two things in great need
If it's two involved,
Then two need to plant the seeds.
You are it for me!
I meant exactly what I said!
Which means even if you leave,
There will only be one in my bed.

My Worth♡

Don't test my pain
Adding to situations of shame.
Yes, I've been married
Not once, not twice, but three.
And yes, the pain I've felt from not 1, not 2, but divorces
are also 3.
I have never been given the easy hand at anything in my life!
So, after every divorce—yes, I had to climb my way out of
that strife!
And just because life looks easy now, doesn't lessen my sacrifice.
How do you want me to applaud your accomplishments?
When Mine—to you—Don't mean Shit!

*** WOW ***

Yeah, that's when reality made me spit!
From deep down in the pit of my stomach
Upon first breath, uttering, "I'm alone again, Dammit!"

No More

When catering is expected as if it's your job;
When thoughtful gestures have long since been forgotten;
When feelings turn cold as ice because needs weren't met;
Well I say, "No more!"
No more wasted time on ungrateful individuals.
No more people pleasing outside your boundaries.
No more putting other's feelings and worries above your own.
Again, I say, "No more!"
No more putting me last to put you first.
No more shelving my emotions to satisfy your insecurities.
No more toning down my awesomeness for your ego.
Now it's about me!
It's not about you...
No More!

Reality Bytes♡

What to do when your thoughts are revealed in opposite
All the while thinking you're top notch.
Reality has a way of biting us when least expected.
Getting bit is currently hurting my flesh.
Knowing facts spoken were from the rest.
DAMN!
If only—for once, I not get knocked down when it counts the most!
Knowing the importance and always demanding the same.
The same given to, but in the moment, not given in return.
Oh, how to roll the time back and un-say what was said!
Well, no such thing!
And what this day has taught me is
Reality Bytes.

Life

A Pain

Pain so deep, it creates a black hole;
Wishing no one would ever have to know.
Hurt from the inside that makes your soul weep;
Trying not to let it ooze and seep
Into places unknown,
Slipping past the bone
To the meat and tissue
Of the issue at hand.
This is something I just can't stand!

Audacity♡

Who told you that you had a right—
A right to grow, to build, to dream?
The Audacity!
"That you think you can own something and make your
 own money,"
Says a voice many aim to no longer hear.
Encouragements freely coming from people you've just met.
Welcoming arms surround you
While emerging yourself in a New Atmosphere;
An atmosphere of success, of joy, of hope.
So again, I ask,
Who gave you The Audacity to think so highly of yourself
That you place yourself on a pedestal
Not to be knocked down ever again.
Who are you?

I AM ME!

Be the Dream

Live to love.
Love to grow.
Learn to teach.
Teach to know.
Know to build.
Build to own.
Own to live.
Live to love.

Life gives air to Dreams
While dreaming of the life you own.
Live your goals and earn your happiness—
Happiness in Life!
And life is love.
Love yourself…
For yourself.

Bounce♡

Don't thank me when you think I need it.
Fake smiling at me just to feel connected.
Missed meal cramps forcing you to call,
Not really wanting to, but knowing it's needed.
Still attempting to use me until you hit your expiration date.
Bounce.
Why?
I was made and now created to be something more than
most…believed.
Smiling at my failures while watching from afar at the
paths I take.
Spying, as if it's a job done professionally, All While Free!
Bounce.
Who made you think to put a price on my dreams?
Don't think to limit my growth—Bounce!
Bounce, and watch how high I soar.
Bounce, and watch how bright my crown shine!
But see, my dreams won't let me dream, alone.
So, you can
Bounce off that negative train you've been riding.
Bounce, and climb with me.
And not on my back or in the shadows.
Bounce! Together! United!

Captured Feelings♡

There are times in life that you wish could be on repeat.
Repeat, because they were so glorious and amazing
That you just wanted to relive and capture the feelings
that went along with it.
If life was on repeat, there would be no elevation!
There would be no growth.
There would be no progress.
We would never have the opportunity to
Transform into the Wonderful Magnificent Human Beings
Filled with love and happiness!

Choosy Losers

Choosy Losers
Choose me when all choices are closed.
Making decisions like you proposed.
Proposed something more than death.
Reaching inside my soul,
Snatching out my breath

You Soul Stealing Loser, You!
Release me, before you find
Blue, black, and purple marks all around
Catching this universal beat down!

Find yourself and turn me LOOSE!
You silly, silly, silly goose!

Silly be damned!
Asking is now out the door.
Don't come 'round here anymore!
I swore I would remain free.
I didn't need you to agree.
Why??
Because the Choosy Losers,
Chose for me.

Dreaming

Hot from the fire, black from the flames;
You hurled blazing daggers at the mention of my name.
Running for shade, afraid to see light;
Knowing all along, you weren't right.
To tell lies and pass them off as truth;
Here's the microphone, get in the booth.
And get the facts straight for all to hear.
Yeah, I know I'm dreaming.
You won't make it clear.
To do as desired, would make you in the wrong.
With repeat lyrics "You're always right" playing your
favorite song.

Experiences♡

Feelings you receive from your daily out and about
lifestyles and responsibilities;
These are unknowingly released when you settle down
for the day.
Be conscious of atmospheres you enter into while on your
traveling way.
Energy sticks to you like clothes.
Not releasing its grip until showered off.
Only then can you move through your space
In PEACE and turn the power off, to chill.
Cleansing your Mind, Body and Spirit
Before or as you enter your domain
Is of the UTMOST IMPORTANCE
To experience.

For Real or For Fake

Some things in life are usually put into categories that are relatable. Figure out if it's for real or for fake.

For Real – This is when you know it's genuine. These are the things that came from the heart! It's when it's given freely and not expected to be returned or replaced. In some ways this comes from a positive place that only sets the positivity train in motion.

For Fake – This can definitely look like the real thing but, feeling very different in the end. These leave expectations that can never be fulfilled or replaced. Given with a partially honest thought, but with comments and motions that make you not want such from that person, again because it cost you too much.

Too much of your peace and your patience.

So, take your time in creating your private circle.

When deciding, always pick *you*.

You are what's needed for your "life's reel" to come true for You!

Happy Happy, Joy Joy♡

What's the saying the elders used to use in a sarcastic way?
"Happy Happy, Joy Joy" is what they'd say.
Just letting you know they hear you,
But with no dedication to the conversation at hand.
Clearly giving you the floor to unknowingly entertain the extended family.
But making sure to "stay in a kid's place," as a child should.
You see, these simple events have played out over and again with time,
But the stories they left us with is what should continue to flow.
So, years from now when you hear it,
I know I've added to the art in the telling of
One of my Happy Happy, Joy Joy parts.

Haters♡

Create what you feel;
Feeling in your style.
Go with the flow.
Glide on your heels.
Own every choice you make.
Claim your peace.
Don't settle for less.
That's not your feat.
Say what you want about me climbing a bigger tree.
Show me who you are and I'll show you who you wanna be.
Don't hate at the expressions coming out.
Join the team, give a shout!
Blow me with the breeze only you can provide,
Storing the rest, not showing the inside.
It's alright, I've seen what I needed to see.
So, let bygones be bygones and leave me be.
Allowing the universe to shape and mold
My mind to handle and hold
Tight to all that's headed this way.
"Thank you. Thank you. Thank you, Haters,"
Is all I can say.

Inspiration♡

Watching you do your thang.
Ready to fly with new wings.
Who knew the direction this was headed?
Not me! It was always something I dreaded.
Being on stage for everyone to stare
With all the smiles, I'd find the glare.
The one that puts me in an uncomfortable space
Demanding I stand strong and take my place
At the spot given for me to shine.
Nah, I can't sit down this time.
Not when it's so much involved
And too many pieces left to solve.

O.P.P.

What are your thoughts when you pose in your style?
Show me!
Then show them your favorable side.
Don't turn away or hide.
Trust that I'll have your backside.

You give new light and expression that makes words and pictures
An actual confession;
A value not easily displayed, with such subtle aggression.
Track lighting tracking down your spine;
Brightening your skin, adding to the fine lines
In favor of your aura.
Watch out world as I roll into my prime!
"I get it from my momma" is how the saying goes,
But in the end—who really knows?
You're given a life to blaze a trail,
Not to cower down, shrinking only to fail.
Add the sails of that ship to your scale
In favor of your Original Posse Pose!

Personalities

When emotions change or become too much to handle,
What are you to do?
Do you run and cry, while waiting it out?
Hopefully your coping mechanisms are working, but if not,
Here is something to grasp.
Through my experiences, I've noticed that different situations create a different side.
Why is that, you ask?
Because, I've developed different personalities to hide.
Right now, I have four, but who knows the final number?
Yes, I caught your sideways look on the slide.
But, what I'm meaning to do is share an epiphany with you.
I've lived with myself all my life!
And no one should know me better, right?
Well, I didn't discover such on my own.
It was actually brought to my foresight,
Hanging on to a statement, phenomenal at best.
And left there hanging with all the rest.
In closing, I hope that this will elevate someone else's troubles like it did for me.
You see, being able to categorize who handles what, makes my life and
Understanding flow evenly.
So, the word for the day is,
"Don't be like Mike, don't even be like me."
Just make sure to be,
All sides of you…
Equally.

Quiet Storm

Wind blowing wildly in reckless abandon.
Trash sending warning signs along the streets.
Traveling in organized patterns to
Destinations unknown.
People hunkering down
To get from Point A to Point B.
Where did all this come from, you ask?
Did the weatherman miss the mark?
Or did we do something to disapprove?
Maybe it's not meant for us to know
All of Mother Nature's moves.
But see,
This one.
This one will refuse to conform,
For she, she is rightfully named...
Quiet Storm.

Roll Modeling♡

What does it mean to be admired
When someone looks up to you?
If we don't become the standards
Then who has a clue?
Tell them words that's positive, and watch them grow.
Soaring high in knowledge and grace
To their rightful place.
Let's clear the space and make a way
For all of our youth today.
Build the bridges for the ride.
Make them comfortable inside.
Roll.
Shine.
Take Pride in the Gift and Sift the Flavor
Of what's to come!

Self Sync♡

The feel of my heart beats sometimes too fast.

The only way I can catch my breath is when I open my eyes.

To have your eyes open while also listening to the beat
Can be distracting,
Because while the beat is steady,
It is continually opening.

When your beats open your heart more than your eyes,
You can find yourself in a delicate situation.

Knowing the balance is key.
Learning the balance is art.
Working your rhythm equals your sight and emotions.

Know your balance.
Learn your rhythm.

This beat is yours and yours alone.

Solace

Relaxing on the lake while others fish;
Daydreaming about solace and happiness.
This is when family becomes exactly what is required;
Glad that I'm retired.
I've been about getting on track.
Wonderful nature walks, enjoyable boat rides;
Parking in the middle of nowhere to get my thoughts correct.
This is Priority—self.
Something that will never change.
She is my solid solace.

Take a Breath♡

Life to me has been a crazy whirlwind.
I've had ultimate lows to my body and my mind.
I've been tested for just having a voice that refuses to quiet.
My personality **pops** loud, just to be heard.
All while second-guessing most major decisions made.
Blindly seeking the happiness, I know in my soul,
I Deserve.
Take a breath.
Move.
Because someone made promises
Causing an end, desperately needed.
Take a breath.
Phone rings.
A voice I haven't heard aggressively speaks to me.
Words spoken so bold, I listen.
Recognition hits as I start to remember the past.
I
Take
A
Breath.
And then, I remember to keep breathing
Because life now
Tastes
So
Good
That I have to remember to
Take…
A…
Breath.

That's Enough♡

How do you know when to tell someone you've had ENOUGH?
When you're being picked on and singled out.
When the stress has you in tears at work.
When your appetite is so confused—no food is tasty.
This is when you decide what's important to you.
Don't let anyone change the way you operate when you've done nothing wrong.
Your only responsibility is being true
To the natural you.

Thicker than Blood♡

Being looked over by ones you hold dear and near.

To desire so strong, it alters your personality.

What's the word to express without increasing the agitation?

Agitation so deep, the thought causes violent reactions – from within.

Can't eat, sleep is scarce.

Breath comes baited.

Thoughts turn tainted from injury–

Injuries that go beyond the physical to Hurt my Soul!

That's the cause of the stress

Attempting to maneuver while diligently

Searching for the positivity necessary for our future.

The need to feel wanted is thicker than blood.

This need restructures the sweet words directed your way.

Everything gets so choppy that

The need to be alone, on my own – is warranted.

Not just warranted – needed – necessary–desired!

Never make the ones you love feel anything less than important…

Especially from you.

Twisted Turns♡

Life comes with risks.
Lessons arrive in curves.
Roads bend and twist.
Some say, "That shit's for the birds."
Such knowledge is unable to be retained.
But learning the lessons that life gives,
Usually leaves much more than stains.
Brain power used on unnecessary things
Have you totally losing your mind.
While training our steps to follow the guides,
Telling you you're on the wrong side.
Ride your road--whether bumpy or paved—
And store your life's lessons
In the file labeled—
Saved.

Vocals Needed♡

What to make of a deep sigh;
When questions asked, float away on the wind.
Wind carrying answers—wanting to be heard;
Needing the validation required to continue.

While continuing on the path life deems necessary;
Necessary to move. To breathe. To love. To grow.
Growth that spreads to every aspect of your world.

The world that you have surrounded yourself with.
So, exhale and let your words be heard.
Someone needs to hear it!
Don't let a deep sigh stop your voice.
Your vocals are needed.

Warm Up

I'm a little shy…
At least until I warm up.
So, for those who really know me
Know sometimes it's hard to keep up.
But that's not a worry for now.
Well, at least
Until I
Warm up.

What Kind

What kind of people are we that only some listen to warnings?
What kind of people are we when you can't help another in need?
What kind of people are we, when animals are treated better than some family?
What kind of people are we when we appear as beggars for stuff we don't need?
Well, to answer your question,
We are human people.
People of individual thoughts, actions, motives, and things of importance.
We were created equal,
But it's the differences that divide us.
So, where does that leave us?
I say it still leaves us as humans.
Some deserving, some undeserving.
We should strive to be the best human beings we can.

Who am I

Who am I or who is she?
Who is this person that's been staring back at me from time to time?
Am I Mother Nature, because I am feeling the seasons?
When it's raining—the gloominess inside—is so overwhelming.
Funny thing is, prior to now, rains had quite a different effect.
How do I manage these internal changes from the seasonal storms,
When the wind won't allow time to label them as they are?
Could it be maturity, preparing me for my older years?
Who am I or who is She?
That's a great question.
Besides the name, the woman writing this poem,
She isn't under my thumb.
So to answer this question would be a lie!
She is not defined!
She is still developing in this current seasonal storm.

Why Me

"Why me?" is a question asked quite often.
No one feels as if they should have to be the One to deal with certain things.
"Why me?" is asked when finding yourself in sticky situations that end—ugly.
"Why me? Why me? Why me?"
The question is asked repeatedly, never really realizing the asked question is wrong.
"Why *not* me?" Is answered when you start to build the confidence within.
When your back bone is straightened by the pride at which you carry yourself.
"Why not me?" is the answer when you begin to hear the strength in your voice,
Carried by the powerful words spoken.
"Why not me?"
I am strong!
I am beautiful!
I am smart!
I am a warrior!
"Why not me?"
Me, who was built for endurance, pride, strength, and foundation.
Such resilience goes beyond words.
So here I am,
No longer asking, "Why me?" but instead
Learning how to declare the VICTORY!

About the Author

Alee J. was born in Mt. Clemens, MI. She is the second oldest of eight siblings, and has mother/daughter/sister love to many non-blood bonded.

Alee J. is a retired Detroit Police Officer and Massage Therapist. With such a high energy level, she is always discovering and creating new things, sparking AleeJDesigns.com, where original crochet accessories are all handmade by Alee J.

Poetry has been a love of Alee J.'s for many years, progressing with age and experience. It has been a healing form of expression, along with journaling.

Through this view into her life, Alee J.'s desire is that her words aren't just read, repeated and put away...No! Alee J. wants you to "Feel Her."

CPSIA information can be obtained
at www.ICGtesting.com
Printed in the USA
JSHW021646240922
30779JS00002B/6